OK, BOOMER

and other age–

(in)appropriate

JOKES

LISA BETH JOHNSON AND PHOEBE BOTTOMS

San Diego, California

Portable Press
An imprint of Printers Row Publishing Group
10350 Barnes Canyon Road, Suite 100, San Diego, CA 92121
www.portablepress.com • mail@portablepress.com

Printers Row Publishing Group is a division of Readerlink
Distribution Services, LLC.
Portable Press is a registered trademark of Readerlink
Distribution Services, LLC.

Correspondence regarding the content of this book
should be sent to Portable Press, Editorial Department,
at the above address.

Publisher: Peter Norton • Associate Publisher: Ana Parker
Senior Developmental Editor: April Graham Farr
Production Team: Julie Greene, Rusty von Dyl

Library of Congress Control Number: 2020934954
ISBN: 978-1-64517-520-9

Printed in the United States of America

24 23 22 21 20   1 2 3 4 5

An Introduction

OK, Boomer . . . so you purchased this book, a physical book that you can actually smell (take a moment to sniff the fresh glue) and hold in your hands (how fun is it to just flip through the pages?). Well, congratulations! That's very on brand for you!

You also bought a book named after a meme[1] in which you, Baby Boomer,[2] are the butt of the joke. The youth of today[3] can't look up from their phones long enough to roll their eyes at you IRL,[4] so they've created the ultimate verbal eye roll: "OK, Boomer . . ."

Is it funny? That's not really the point. Is it clever? Also not the point. Does it get under your skin to know that the younger generations find the older ones out of touch and to blame for all the ills they see in the world? *That's* the point.

---

[1] An online medium—video, text, or image—that gets copied, added to, and spread around on the internet like a bad rash . . . or any rash, I suppose.

[2] Baby Boomers were born between 1946 and 1964.

[3] Millennials were born between 1981 and 1996; Generation Z, between 1997 and now. Generation X came between 1965 and 1980 but live a little too close to the house to throw rocks.

[4] IRL=in real life.

Here's a joke: Past, Present, and Future walk into a bar . . . and then things get *tense*. Funny joke if you're a fan of grammar humor,[5] but it also reminds us that time is a concept that comes with some baggage.

We are each born into a particular era and must immediately contend with the lovable idiots who came before us. We roll our eyes at their ways and then have only the briefest of moments to consider and implement a better plan. As soon as we stand back to take a look at our masterpiece, a bunch of kids come along and roll their eyes at *us*!

Although you're reading this on a printed page—technology more than a millennium old—it's during times of

[5] The three main tenses of verbs are past, present, and future; for example: "boomed," "booms," "will boom."

huge technological and social advancements that things get *the most* eye roll-y between generations. And if there's one thing we can probably all agree on, it's that the last hundred years have honestly been *a lot*.

So how do we deal with the dismissive attitudes of our thoroughly and disgustingly modern youth? The self-righteous finger wagging of our elders? With the time-honored tradition of humor. It's the one thing we all hope to continue passing on to future generations for as long as that's possible.

Oh, and to all the non-Boomers who picked up this book: I know, I know. [6]

---

[6] TL;DR=Too long; didn't read.

Boomers say kids don't even know
what books are anymore—but if we're
considering *this* a book,
maybe that's a good thing!

~~~~~~~~~~~~~~~~~~~~~~~~~~~~~~~~

Boomer:
"Have you seen that news story about . . ."

Everyone:
"OMG please check Snopes first. We'll wait."

Quiz: Which Generation Are You?

A Boomer is 30 minutes into a "What a small world!" story that doesn't look like it's ever going to end. What do you do?

A. Say you have to go check on the kids. Thank God you had them, because they're the perfect excuse for not listening to that same story you've already heard a million times.

B. Look at your phone and don't look up no matter what. Eye contact only encourages a Boomer.

C. Zone out while you try to imagine what it was like to have a phone attached to a wall.

(Answers: A. Gen X; B. Millennial; C. Gen Z)

Things That Still Exist Only Because of Boomers

basic cable
blouses
buffets
checks
coupons
cruises
cursive
email scams
Facebook
HSN and QVC
infomercials
mayo salads
metal detectors
milk
newspapers
pencils
phone books
potpourri
Reader's Digest
the word "slacks"
sweepstakes
talk radio
USPS
Wheel of Fortune
Yahoo!

sammi
@samkru_

You millennials and your obsession with public healthcare. Back in my day we just died

~~~~~~~~~~~~~~~~~~~~~~~~~~~~~

OK, Boomer . . . "It is what it is"
is pretty much what got us here!

OK, Boomer . . . I just spent 30 minutes over Skype trying to help you set up your new smart TV before realizing you've been punching microwave buttons this whole time.

~~~~~~~~~~~~~~~~~~~~~~~~~~~~~~

Gen X also learned to program when they were young . . . but it was mostly just the VCR.

Boomer: "Back in my day we had beatniks!"

Gen Xer: "Are there still goth kids?"

Millennial: "No, they're emo."

Gen Zer: "That's just all of us now."

"If you're not offended then
you're not paying attention!"
—Millennial elders

"Why are you so offended by everything?"
—also Millennial elders

~~~~~~~~~~~~~~~~~~~~~~~~~~~~~~

A Boomer walks into a bar—uphill, both ways.

Q: How many Boomers does it take to change a lightbulb?

A: Three: one to do it, and two to talk about how much better the old one was.

Q: How many Boomers does it take to change a lightbulb?

A: There's an app for that now, Grandpa.

OK, Boomer . . . Millennials *should* spend less
on brunch—just like they should have spent
more on time travel and betting on past
Super Bowls to pay off their student loans.

~~~~~~~~~~~~~~~~~~~~~~~~~~~~~~~~~~~~~~

Boomers tried to make fun of their elders too,
but "OK, the Greatest Generation . . ."
just doesn't have the same ring to it.

Boomer:
"Satan? Is that even a food?"

Gen Xer:
"'Say-shan,' I think it's pronounced?"

Millennial:
"I can't eat that. It's made of wheat gluten."

Gen Zer:
(plays a YouTube video that demonstrates
pronunciation of "seitan" vegan meat)

Rare photograph of the
last known Millennial
to have never published
an online selfie!

My Boomer parents hate my politics, but they paid *a lot* in tuition so I could be "out of touch with the electorate."

~~~~~~

A grandfather thinks TikTok is an app used to tell time. It kind of is, because that definitely tells us how old he is.

How Gen X Employees Can Get Ahead

1. Create a fake government website announcing free money for retired Boomers. Show to Boomer bosses and watch everything fall into place.

2. Continue to go get drinks with younger coworkers, but also don't forget to attend your AA meetings.

3. Make fun of LinkedIn but then keep updating yours. Who knows, maybe someday it will finally pay off.

4. Have a sense of humor about yourself. You can cry about being teased once you get home.

Gen Z is already bored with "OK, Boomer" and has come up with a new way to dismiss another demographic. Meet Karen!

Who is Karen? A middle-aged Gen X woman, usually a mom.

Karen has "I want to speak to your manager" hair.

Karen tells a cashier, "I can't believe you have to work on Christmas" with a sad smile, but then tries to get that same cashier fired for not saying "thank you" to her.

OK, Boomer . . . younger generations are bad at
face-to-face talking, but telling "female driver"
jokes at the dinner table isn't really a conversation.
Also, Mom told me to tell you she's pissed.

Gen Zers just hope they make it long
enough to be supremely insufferable
to younger generations.

~~~~~~~~~~~~~~~~~~~~~~~~~~~~~~~~~~~~~

Millennial: "What does AOL stand for?
I'm guessing it's 'all older ladies'?"

Baby Boomers love to tell you not to
look at your phone so much . . .
and to tell you that in a
twelve-paragraph long text.

~~~~~~~~~~~~~~~~~~~~~~~~~~~~~~~~~~~~~~~

Q: What's a Baby Boomer's favorite book?

A:

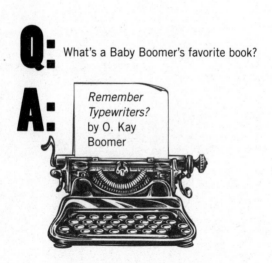

*Remember
Typewriters?*
by O. Kay
Boomer

"Saying 'OK, Boomer' in the workplace is age discrimination but putting 'Now Hiring Happy People' on a recruitment flier isn't?" —Gen Zer

~~~~~~~~~~~~~~~~~~~~~~~~

**OK, Boomer . . . this is what your
Google search history says:**

Carol! Call me! How do I get Carol to call me?
What's cool now?
Google search

Boomers buy fuel-efficient cars to save gas money;
Millennials buy them to save the world.

~~~~~~

"Tofu has no personality, which is why people
who eat it don't either." OK, Boomer . . . does
eating wings for every meal explain why you're
such a chicken when it comes to trying anything new?

Boomer:
"I remember where I was when I found
out Kennedy was shot."

Gen Xer:
"I remember where I was when I
found out the Challenger exploded."

Millennial:
"I remember where I was when 9/11 happened."

Gen Zer:
"Where was I when something awful happened
in the news? Hmm . . . not sure I can remember
where I've been *every day* for the last 18 years."

Toby SnowWolf
@303SnowWolf

Boomer culture is saying "wow, how ever do you afford $11 for Hulu?" when they sit there watching $60 / month cable TV talking on a $40 / month landline phone.

~~~~~~~~~~~~~~~~~~~~~~~~~~~~~~~

OK, Boomer . . .
we love our
kale, it's true.
But you guys tried
to make ketchup
a vegetable.

Conversation Topics for Gen Xers

How many flannels and ripped jeans they had
(and do they still have them? Because they're back)

How cool MTV *used* to be (it was fine)

Lollapalooza (did they really go to all of them,
and how would they even remember?)

Being latchkey kids (in an era that *also*
had the most serial killers)

OK, Boomer . . . I get it, sometimes the internet is confusing. For instance, yesterday I didn't go on Reddit and today I logged in and can't understand *any* of the memes.

~~~~~~~~~~~~~~~~~~~~~~~~~~~~~

If "K" is now an abbreviation for "OK," maybe "K-pop" could be an abbreviation for "OK, Boomer."

Gen Zer:
"OK, Boomer . . . If you can't
handle me at my worst, you
don't deserve me at my best!"

Boomer:
". . . you have a best?"

Statistics have shown that Baby Boomers
spend at least 15 hours per week
online . . . although to be fair,
14 of those are spent trying
to remember their passwords.

~~~~~~~~~~~~~~~~~~~~~~~~~~~~~~~~~~

Q: What do you say to a Boomer who is
mad at you for saying, "OK, Boomer"?

A: "Rub some dirt on it!"

A Gen-X Karen:
"This place has the worst coffee
I've ever had in my life!"

Millennial barista:
*puts a new sign in front of store reading
"Come on in and try the worst coffee one
Karen has ever had in her whole entire life!"*

OK, Boomer . . . I *will* go ahead
and "ask the Googles."

~~~~~~~~~~~~~~~~~~~~~~~~~~~~~~~~~~

The Greatest Generation created the
Silent Generation. I'm assuming they're
called "greatest" because anyone who
can keep their kids silent must be.

Gen Z snowflakes are complaining
about having to take shelter in their
houses because of COVID-19.

When I was in school, we were told
to "duck-and-cover" under a desk
in the event of an atomic bomb.

~~~~~~~~~~~~~~~~~~~~~~~~~~~~~~~~~~~~~

 Kevin
@KevOnStage

Dad Joke: How do you weigh a millennial?
In InstaGrams

Grams are a measure of weight and Instagram
is a measure of clout. Get it?

Match the Font with the Generation

Scrolly cursive (think anything written on distressed-wood wall decor):
Boomers

Heavy metal font (they doodled *a lot*):
Generation X

Something sans serif (brunch chalkboard font):
Millennials

A series of emojis followed by multiple vowels:
Generation Z

Millennials drink less and have sex less
than previous generations? No wonder
they think everything is awful!

~~~~~~~~~~~~~~~~~~~~~~~~~~~~~~~

Boomer:
"I can't believe you eat sushi.
It's so weird and slimy."

Also Boomer:
"I'm making SPAM burgers with
ranch-packet seasoning!"

It's going to be fun to see how future
generations piss off Gen Z by trying to
remake their favorite YouTube channels.

~~~~~~~~~~~~~~~~~~~~~~~~~~~~~~~~~~~~~~~

OK, Boomer . . . yes, I did just take a selfie
at Versailles, but have you seen how self-absorbed
the people who built this place were?

Before you start hating on Gen Z, remember that most of your loved and cherished pets are in that same age bracket!

The rules for being a member of Gen X are the same rules for being in *Fight Club*.

Millennials blame Boomers for everything,
but their most valid complaint is that they
put *carpet* over *so many beautiful hardwood floors*!

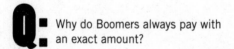

Q: Why do Boomers always pay with
an exact amount?

A: Because they're afraid of change.

Waiter: "Hello. What can I get you?"

Woman: "One lukewarm water with no ice and lemon—oh, and extra lemon."

Man: "And do you have any bread—I can't have butter, do you have margarine? But it has to be soft!"

Waiter: "OK, Boomers . . ."

What Kind of House Can Each Generation Afford?

Boomer:
soulless McMansion

Gen Xer:
old house with character they have to rent
out in order to afford the mortgage

Millennial:
van down by the river . . . but it's styled to the hilt

Gen Zer:
will never leave their parents' house until
civilization collapses, and even then . . .

OK, Boomer . . . some of you really love
Rush the band and some of you really
love Rush the Limbaugh.

~~~~~~

Boomer definition: "Tipping" means
telling the waiter how they could have done
their job better, and then not giving a
tip in order to "build character."

A study said the number one issue Boomers have with Millennials is their complaining—but the study didn't mention that the list went to 1,230,482.

That same study found that, for Millennials, Boomers complaining about them was issue number one in 2,934.

~~~~~~~~~~~~~~~~~~~~~~~~~~~~~~~~~~~~~

"Fidget spinners? Fidget spinning was illegal in 43 states when I was growing up!"
"OK, Boomer."

giabuchi
@jaboukie

"hey just following up"

-unemployed millennial proverb

~~~~~~~~~~~~~~~~~~~~~~~~

I wish Gen Z loved anything as
much as Boomers love Viagra jokes.

OK, Boomer . . . I stopped reading your email after the line "Someone I know shared this on Facebook . . ."

~~~~~~

My dad always tries to answer phone calls with his smart watch. On a related note, I've run out of ways to say "Fitbits don't do that."

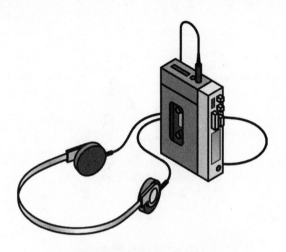

Things That Don't Exist Anymore Because Gen X Loves to Adopt New Technology but Still Get Nostalgic AF

Sony Walkman

cordless landlines

pagers

answering machines

Prozac

Dog Generations

"Rin Tin Tin . . . now *that* was
the greatest generation."

"No, Rin Tin Tin was very problematic.
Lassie actually tried to warn people about things
and make the world better!"

"Yeah, but Lassie isn't representative of all dogs.
Benji was a mutt—*that's* a *real* dog of the people!"

"Dogs nowadays don't understand hard work.
All they want is to do something cute or stupid
to get on the internet!"

OK, Boomer . . . your memes are like if a Grandpa thought "dad jokes" were *way* too edgy.

~~~~~~~~~~~~~~~~~~~~~~~~~~~~~~~~~~~~~~~

"A wise man once said that if you don't stand for something, you'll fall for anything." OK, Boomer . . . but last week you emailed me a letter from a Nigerian prince, a Photoshopped news story, and three viruses.

Nearly Extinct Boomer Sounds

an electronic calculator printing the total

a rotary dial turning back to zero

"You've got mail!"

Wayne Newton

"Social security" is knowing that
younger generations can say, "OK, Boomer"
to you and it doesn't even bother you.

~~~~~~~~~~~~~~~~~~~~~~~~~~~~~~~~~~~~

"Being a teen is cool . . . but it's even cooler
once you're in your 40s!" —Gen Xer

OK, Boomer . . . the sea levels are rising
but some young person's jeans falling below
hip level is a devastating national emergency.

~~~~~~~~~~~~~~~~~~~~~~~~~~~~~~~~~~~~

If I had a dollar for every time a Boomer
told me how much their first house cost,
I'd almost have enough to pay rent on the studio
apartment I share with eight other working adults.

Gen Xer:
"Want to get something to drink?"

Gen Zer:
"You're thirsty!"

Gen Xer:
"Yeah, I know . . . that's why I asked."

Gen Zer:
"Salty!"

Boomer:
(slowly blinks and walks away)

Boomers whisper the word "therapist" . . .
Millennials and Gen Zers post
Snapchats of their sessions.

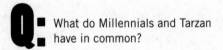

Q: What do Millennials and Tarzan
have in common?

A: Sometimes they both "miss Vine."

OK, Boomer, TikTok is like Vine if you . . .

OK, Boomer, Vine is like Instagram if you . . .

OK, Boomer, Instagram is like Twitter if you . . .

OK, Boomer, Twitter is like Facebook if you . . .

~~~~~~

Make fun of your grandparents' lack of tech
savvy all you want, Gen Z, but can you even
name all the ingredients in bread?

Ways to Wake Up Your Gen X Boss if There's No More Coffee

Play Montell Jordan "This Is How We Do It"

Sell them some of your Adderall prescription

Say "OK, Boomer!" to them and they'll
go into beast mode

It's a trick question. There's always coffee.
That's Gen X's greatest contribution to the world.

OK, Boomer . . . if none of us respects
the past or dresses well, then explain why
we're the first generation since your
parents to bring back the fedora?

~~~~~~~~~~~~~~~~~~~~~~~~~~

I want to live long enough to see
if Gen Z continues to use their slang
when they're grandparents.

My Boomer grandmother just started dating online and asked me what the eggplant and peach emojis mean. I told her it means "vegetarians," so now she responds, "I HATE 🍆 🍑 !" to any potential dates.
All is right in the world again.

~~~~~~

If a tree falls in the forest and no one is around to make an Instagram story of it, did it even happen?

Earlier Generational Divides

"New machines are killing the weaving industry!"
"OK, Loomer."

"Women should only wear dresses!"
"OK, Bloomer."

"When I was young, serfs worked the land!"
"OK, Ruler."

Boomers try to freak out their neighbors
by naming their Wi-Fi "FBI Surveillance Van 7,"
but Millennials try to freak out their neighbors by
naming theirs "Pansexual Vegan Who Votes 69."

~~~~~~

The Silent Generation is said to have worked hard
without complaint. But they never had to wait three
whole minutes for a Netflix show to buffer.

OK, Boomer . . . I know you think the name
Trevin is stupid, but 20 of the most
popular names the year you were born
were all variations of "Michael."

Of course Millennials got participation trophies . . .
Gen Xers slacked so hard that everyone got
excited the first time Millennials
signed up for *anything*!

Lucy Bryan
@lucy__bryan

Baby boomer culture is making fun of people who go to Starbucks but also making fun of people who go to small locally owned coffee shops

~~~~~~~~~~~~~~~~~~~~~~~~~~~~~~~~~~~

If you think young people are ruining comedy
but feel personally slighted over "OK, Boomer,"
I've got a mirror over here I'd like you to look into.

I just found out even the *term* "Generation X"
was initially intended for Baby Boomers,
but they rejected it for sounding "too edgy."

~~~~~~~~~~~~~~~~~~~~~~~~~~~~~~~~

Q: What's a Millennial's favorite fragrance?

A: Scents of Entitlement

Boomers:
"Snow in July? Where's your 'global warming' now, kids?"

Gen X:
"Remember when we all tried to save the whales? That was cool."

Millennials:
"How are you *just now* getting a sense of urgency about this?"

Gen Z:
"I'm more interested in what any child has to say on this subject than any of you adults."

OK, Boomer . . . it seems crazy for you to think
that I was born after 2001, but do you see how
crazy it is for me to wrap my head around the fact
that you were born before the Beatles?

~~~~~~~~~~~~~~~~~~~~~~~~~~~~~~~~~~~

It's true that Millennials are known to cry more
at work than previous generations . . . but that's
because the Boomers won't retire and the
Karens are always trying to get them fired.

Common Health Issues
of Each Generation

Boomers:
Chronic tunnel vision; stress from trying to provide for every living generation before or since them.

Gen Xers:
Any ailment you could get from not having health care from age 18 to the 2010 passage of ACA.

Millennials:
Webbed hands from too much texting—but on the bright side, that will make it easier to swim through the flooded cities of the future!

Gen Zers:
"Air head" syndrome because 20 percent of them have AirPods permanently lodged in their ears and high blood pressure from not saying, "OK, Boomer . . ." every time they think it.

More new Millennial dads are taking time off when their children are born, which is a change for the better: Boomers thought "paternity leave" was when your dad said good-bye and then started a new family across town.

~~~~~~~~~~~~~~~~~~~~~~~~~~

I'm writing a book to help bridge the generational divide called *I'm OK, Boomer . . . You're OK, Boomer.*

OK, Boomer . . . I guess "OK, Boomer" kind of proves the study that only 19 percent of young adults agree that being "respectful" is "important."

~~~~~~~~~~~~~~~~~~~~~~~~~~~~~~~~~~

Every time a Boomer parent comments, "Don't forget we're having dinner with Grandma tonight!" under their kid's selfie, a Millennial invents another social-media app.

Boomer:
"You have to 'act first and apologize later'
to get anything done."

Gen Z:
"But you've never apologized for anything."

Boomer:
"I would if I'd ever been wrong about anything."

Gen Z:
"OOOOOK, Boomer . . ."

Gen Z Social Stressors

Finding the right GIF to send in a group
chat before someone changes the subject

Three dots ... ... then nothing

When Mom joins Snapchat

When they have to lie and say, "Sorry!
Just now seeing this!"

When Dad says he's "adulting"

OK, Boomer . . . you realize bragging about how much money you have in response to someone saying "OK, Boomer" is the *most* "OK, Boomer" thing?

~~~~~~

It's easy to relate to Gen Xers! All you have to do is make sure you've seen every movie and TV show from the 1970s and '80s and have listened to every song ever recorded on vinyl.

"OK, Boomer" really hits close to home . . .
because my kids still live here.

~~~~~~

A lot of Gen Zers are learning basic trades such as woodworking because someday the robot overlords might want some nice furniture in their homes. Woodworking skills also make sense for a generation that might have to build an ark in its lifetime.

"Wait . . . who is this? Wilco?"
—Gen Xer listening to any new music

~~~~~~~~~~~~~~~~~~~~~~~~~~~~~~~~~~~~

The percentage of stay-at-home dads has
doubled with Millennials over the past 10 years.
That makes sense . . . home is the one place
they know they won't encounter a Boomer.

When Boomers tell me that I have a meaningless degree, I tell them that anthropology will help me understand their ancient culture.

~~~~~~~~~~~~~~~~~~~~~~~~~~~~~~

I'm just a Gen X mom, standing in front of her Gen Z kids, asking them to lie to my Boomer parents about the guest room so they don't try to stay here next week.

How do Boomers Comment on Instagram?

Millennial Friend 1:
So cute!

Millennial Friend 2:
That dress tho.

Millennial Friend 3:
Yaaaaassssss!

Boomer Mom:
Call your dad he can't sign into the movie channel you set up for us we're trying to watch that show Lynn and Daniel told us to watch where that woman is stuck on an island also Lynn and Daniel say hi their son is divorced now you should call him you guys always seemed to get along and it looks like he's keeping the house.

Generational Tattoos

Boomer:
"I was at Woodstock '69!"

Gen Xer:
"I was at Woodstock '99!"

Millennial:
Woodstock from Peanuts

Gen Zer:
No tattoos but did buy stock in wood since it's
going to be a precious commodity soon
due to deforestation

OK, Boomer . . . you can earn our respect
as long as you can be simultaneously
authentic, transparent, purposeful, emotionally
connected, stylish, *and* cool . . . It's not hard!

~~~~~~~~~~~~~~~~~~~~~~~~~~~~~~~~~~

I've never felt more seen than when I heard
my grandmother say, "OK, Boomer" to my dad.

Half of modern two-parent households say
they split household chores equally. The other half
said, "Don't lie to the Pew Research Center!"

I'm so sick of Millennials walking around
like they can't afford to own the place.

diamond geezer
@bigsolidegg

Baby boomer culture is taking the same group picture on 10 different phones instead of sending one photo to each other.

~~~~~~~~~~~~~~~~~~~~~~~~~~~~~~~

OK, Millennial . . . food isn't inherently *healthier* just because you put it all together in a bowl.

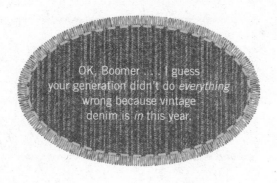

OK, Boomer . . . I guess
your generation didn't do *everything*
wrong because vintage
denim is *in* this year.

~~~~~~~~~~~~~~~~~~~~~~~~~~~

If a Gen Zer asks you why some people in
old photographs have red eyes, tell them
they're too young to remember the
demon uprising of the 1980s.

People say Millennials are entitled,
but have you ever tried to tell a Boomer at
the grocery store that her coupon expired?

~~~~~~~~~~~~~~~~~~~~~~~~~~~~

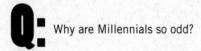

Q: Why are Millennials so odd?

A: Because they can't . . . even . . .

Where Does Each Generation Get Its News?

Boomer:
Facebook posts by the guy in town who sells fishing lures. Tweets from a woman they met at a Mary Kay meeting. Chain emails from that one uncle who moved to the woods.

Gen Xer:
Reads only the headlines of aggregating websites yet seems to have an immediate opinion about the story. Also, TMZ news clips that play on gas station pumps.

Millennial:
Listens to SoundCloud rappers and podcasts started by comedians-turned-bodybuilders.

Gen Zer:
Won't believe anything except a Morse code feed on the dark web from a disgraced whistle-blower.

Just overheard my six-year-old say, "OK, Boomer" to her four-year-old sister, so I think this meme is officially meaningless.

~~~~~~~~~~~~~~~~~~~~~~~~~~~~~~~~~~~~~

OK, Boomer . . . but once you guys are gone, we're gonna switch to the metric system!

What are Gen Z's three biggest fears?

1. Everything that has happened

2. Everything that is happening

3. Everything that will happen

Yoda: "Do or do not. There is no try."
Baby Yoda: "OK, Boomer . . ."

~~~~~~

Boomers who are mad at "OK, Boomer"
need to just do what they've always done:
appropriate it and make it supremely uncool!

OK, Boomer . . . I guess *The Big Chill* wasn't
that bad of a movie because we tried to
remake it . . . and *Thirtysomething* . . . and every
other movie and TV show from your generation.

~~~~~~~~~~~~~~~~~~~~~~~~~~~~~~~~~~~~~~

Boomers used to call it "supply and demand"
when a store went out of business. Now they
call it Millennials' fault.

OK, Boomer . . . eating Tide PODS *is* stupid, but hitchhiking was just a fun, easy way to get around?

"This book is fire!"
—the authors

"Cringy!"
—Gen Zer

Boomer Band/ Millennial Mash-ups

James Taylor Swift
Fleetwood Macklemore
Steve Miller Band of Horses

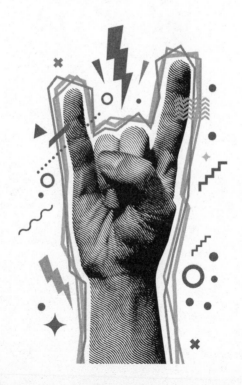

If there's any lesson Boomers should learn from their parents, it's to be sure to spend their remaining years modestly and humbly, so that there's something left for everyone else to inherit.

~~~~~~~~~~~~~~~~~~~~~~~~~~~~~~~~~~~~

OK, Boomer . . . Pokémon *is* kind of basic, but you had a pet rock.

Tinder Pickup Lines for Men of Each Generation

Boomer:
Here's a funny joke about wives
I saw on Facebook.

Gen Xer:
You know, one time I held a boom box outside
my girlfriend's bedroom window . . .

Millennial:
I bought a nice house after I sold an app.

Gen Zer:
Here's a GIF of a hot dog wearing
headphones and yelling.

Law & Order: Special Victims Unit sounds like a mash-up of Nixon-era Boomers and overly sensitive Millennials.

~~~~~~~~~~~~~~~~~~~~~~~~~~~~~~~~~~~~~~~

Ninety percent of people who say "OK, Boomer" are actually Gen Z, and 90 percent of the people they say it to are actually Gen X.

Based on the logic and punctuation,
it wouldn't surprise me if the Russians
are actually making all of those
Baby Boomer memes.

~~~~~~~~~~~~~~~~~~~~~~~~~~~~~

OK, Boomer . . . I switched out your hearing
aid for a suppository. Can you hear
this sh*t we're dealing with now?

Teen:
"I got an F on my paper about
Atlas Shrugged."

Parent:
"What?! I love that book. What did you say?"

Teen:
"OK, Boomer . . ."

Parent:
"No, what did your paper say?"

Teen:
"That's it."

Three Times Boomers
Were Stupider than You

1. Using an iron to straighten their hair

2. Suntanning—with oil!

3. Racing cars without wearing seat belts

~~~~~~~~~~~~~~~~~~~~~~~~~~~~~~~~~~~~~~

Three Times Boomers
Were Smarter than You

1. George Carlin

2. . . . hold on, I'm still thinking!

Are you X, Y, or Z?
Age isn't a number anymore, it's a letter.

~~~~~~

Mad Men proved that younger generations
can look past all the bad things older
generations did . . . provided the older
generations looked really cool doing it.

miranduh
@lackofwizdom

what's your star sign?

i'm a boomer / gen x cusp

~~~~~~~~~~~~~~~~~~~~~~~~~~~

I don't mind if my kids say, "OK, Boomer"
to me because I've been saying,
"whatever, baby" to them
since they were born.

The only thing keeping Gen X from
a full meltdown on Boomers is how
badly they want their record collection.

~~~~~~~~~~~~~~~~~~~~~~~~~~~~~~~~~~

OK, Boomer . . . this fidget spinner gives me
something to do—kind of like how your
generation puts top sheets on beds for no
reason other than to tangle and untangle
yourself out of them.

Gen Z Hamlet:
"To meme or not to meme . . .
there *is* no question!"

Gen Z Boss:
"If you've got time to lean,
you've got time to *meme*!"

~~~~~~~~~~~~~~~~~~~~~~~~~~~~~~~

Read an article that marketers and
the media are ignoring Gen X . . . and
honestly, Gen Xers have never been happier.

"Go outside and get some fresh air!"
OK, Boomer . . . can you turn off your old
pickup truck, muscle car, and motorboat
so we can *have* some fresh air?

~~~~~~~~~~~~~~~~~~~~~~~~~~~~~~~~~~

Q: Why do Millennials type in lowercase?

A: Because they reject capitalism.

Boomers:
ACK!

Gen X:
Not!

Millennials:
Meh...

Gen Z:
(@_@)

~~~~~~~~~~~~~~~~~~~~~~~~~~~~~~~~~

Everyone's "customer service voice" is
the equivalent to baby talk for a Boomer.

Potential Names for Future Generations

Generation Der (GenDer)

Final Girls

Gen AAA

Fish People

~~~~~~~~~~~~~~~~~~~~~~~~~~~~

Be very careful where you
tread next, Millennials . . .
technically Keanu Reeves
is a Baby Boomer.

OK, Boomer . . . *I'm* the snowflake,
but all I did was put boobs on the
snowman and now *you're* offended?

~~~~~~~~~~~~~~~~~~~~~~~~~~~~~~~~

I just asked a Gen Zer to show me something
funny and they showed me a meme that said,
"Laminate your notes so your tears roll off." WTF!

Millennial Shopping List

Himalayan salt rock lamp

charcoal toothpaste

adult coloring books

spiralizer to make zoodles

bath bombs

avocado keeper

sheet masks

Boomers killed the automat.

Gen X killed the two-week vacation.

Millennials killed chain restaurants.

Gen Z is killing Facebook.

Gen TX2000 will kill all obstinate humans.

~~~~~~

When it comes to intergenerational relations,
follow the golden rule: whoever has
the most gold, rules.

Boomers invented modern computer coding but can't decipher what Gen Z's memes mean.

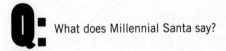

Q: What does Millennial Santa say?

A: "HO HO HO'K, Boomer!"

OK, Boomer . . . the first thing my
generation will do is install robot cashiers
at every store, because no sentient being
deserves listening to Boomer jokes *and* Karen rage.

~~~~~~

A lot of Boomers are nostalgic about the era
they grew up in. But when I die, I hope to
come back as a Millennial's dog.

Gen Zer:
"I love you, Mom. Bet."

Boomer:
"My name is Beth. You should know that.
I'm your mother."

Gen Zer:
"And I oop!"

Boomer:
"Get out of my house, bot!"

Helicopter parenting is a luxury anxiety
for people with too much disposable income.
So I guess a lot of us younger folks are
going to be hands-off!

~~~~~~~~~~~~~~~~~~~~~~~~~~~~~~~~~~

I've seen the way my mom talks to *her* mom,
and it seems to me that "OK, Boomer" is
actually the most mature way any generation
has ever dismissed their elders.

Boomer 1:
"We might have made too many horror movies."

Boomer 2:
"Why do you say that?"

Boomer 1:
"When was the last time anyone
opened their door for you if they
didn't know you were coming over?"

OK, Boomer . . . I know you're not my
sister. I called you "cis."

~~~~~~~~~~~~~~~~~~~~~~~~~~~~~

My parents thought I was reading a
ton of books, because every
time they asked me during a
conversation how I knew something,
I'd say, "Reddit . . ."

OK, Boomer... make your own meme.

First, think of a punch line from a joke you heard 50 years ago. Then, find a picture online that helps set up the punch line. Try Google instead of Facebook—there's actually a lot of stuff on the internet that *isn't* Facebook. Next, send it to everyone whose email you have—even your realtor or a guy you went fishing with 20 years ago. Finally, post it online and get in an unnecessary argument with a distant cousin you haven't seen in more than 30 years.

andrew núñez
@andrew_nunez

millennial culture is texting your mom

"what TIME was i born?"

~~~~~~~~~~~~~~~~~~~~~~~~~~~

Did you hear that they came out with
new Bluetooth earbuds for Boomers?
They're called Grandpods.

Q: How do you make a Gen Xer laugh?

A: Literally any Star Wars pun.

~~~~~~~~~~~~~~~~~~~~~~~~~~~~~~~~

Q: How do you make a Gen Zer laugh?

A: No . . . I'm really asking. I haven't seen my kid smile in 12 years.

OK, Boomer . . . but the proudest *I've*
ever been of my country is in 2018 when
a teen Olympian overslept, lost his coat,
and said f*ck on TV.

~~~~~~~~~~~~~~~~~~~~~~~~~~~~~~~~

OK, Boomer . . . 70 is the new 30.
But if growing up is so bad, why are you
trying to make all of us do it?

OK, everybody . . . there's gonna be a
new generation soon, maybe we can
blame everything on them?

~~~~~~~~~~~~~~~~~~~~~~~~~~~~~~~~~~~~

Gen Z:
"I love this band."

Gen X:
"Oh, they've been around forever. How are
you just now hearing about them?"

Gen Z:
"I *literally* just found out about World War One."

How Do Millennials Spend Their Money?

online associate degree in "memes"

acai bowls

diamond-encrusted fidget spinners

targeted app advertising

Boomers:
Plastic!

Gen X:
Poser!

Millennials:
Extra!

Gen Z:
Fake stan!

~~~~~~~~~~~~~~~~~~~~~~~~~~~~

Fun fact! "Silent Generation" is short
for "Silent but Deadly Generation."

OK, Boomer . . . when I asked if you've
ever rolled a joint, I didn't think you'd
point at your left ankle.

~~~~~~~~~~~~~~~~~~~~~~~~~~~~~~~~~~~~

For every Millennial with college debt,
there's a Baby Boomer making six figures
who can't open a PDF.

Jobs Millennials Don't Want

OK, Boomer . . . the answer
isn't "any job"

but actually, any job

robot repairman
(but . . . we probably won't have a choice)

rancher
(you can't be "on your phone" around cows. Trust)

file clerk
(that 100 percent is the only job available in hell)

OK, Gen Xer... Starter Kit

We get it. You know the lyrics to every
single Weird Al song.

Your teen hair is collectively responsible
for the holes in the ozone layer.

Once you become the old generation, you're gonna be
like the cool uncle and let us do whatever we want!

~~~~~~~~~~~~~~~~~~~~~~~~~~~~~~~~

My grandpa has an app on his phone that
just says "app" and I'm terrified what
will happen if I open it.

I told my parents a friend of mine got rich
inventing an app. They said, "Wow!
Was it some new kind of chicken wing?"

~~~~~~

OK, Gen Zer . . . I don't know how to code, but
when I ask you to wrap your head around the
concept of "burning a CD," steam comes
out of your brain.

OK, Boomer . . . but if I *do* get off of my phone, you'd better make absolutely sure you're ready to talk to me about my favorite YouTube show for the next hour!

~~~~~~~~~~~~~~~~~~~~~~~~~~~

Baby Boomer men love memes about how much their wife annoys them, but it's not OK if *I* say it during dinner?

Boomer meme:
"I'm so old that my train of thought
never leaves the station!"

Gen Z meme:
"My thoughts always lead to a desperate
fight to the death against my peers
over meager resources . . .
like the train in *Hunger Games*!"

Things to Know Before Throwing an Intergenerational Party

Baby Boomer:
Complains about lack of snacks.

Gen Xer:
Brings weird snacks.

Millennial:
Complains about
Boomers not bringing snacks.

Gen Zer:
Will not bring or eat snacks.
Or talk.

One thing we'll never know for sure is
which generation was to blame
for open office spaces.

~~~~~~

For people who supposedly don't
believe in being offended, Boomers sure
do write a lot of letters to their local
news stations about how the
weather women dress.

Healthy meal for a Millennial:
kale foam with alkalized chia pudding
and organic tempeh nuggets.

Healthy meal for a Boomer:
red meat, white starch,
green Jell-O with canned fruit.

I told my grandmother and her friends
that I was elected the mayor of Wi-Fi
and now I get all the freshest cookies.

~~~~~~

OK, Gen Xer . . . you still think
1990 was ten years ago.

Millennials:
"These iPhones are
made in sweatshops!"

Boomers:
"I sweat whenever I have
to shop for an iPhone!"

ZINEQUEST
@tinygorgon

the millennial version of 2.5 kids and a picket

fence is six houseplants and no roommate

~~~~~~

OK, Boomer. This was fun.

Image Credits